SUPER-CHARGED!

DREAM CARS

BY

Jack C. Harris

EDITED BY

Michael E. Goodman

PUBLISHED BY

CRESTWOOD HOUSE

NEW YORK

INDIANA STATE UNIVERSITY LIBRARY

LIBRARY OF CONGRESS CATALOGING IN PUBLICATION DATA

Harris, Jack C. (Jack Carroll)
   Dream cars

   (Super-charged!)
   Includes index.
   SUMMARY: Discusses the history of automobile invention, possible alternative power sources such as electricity and steam, and future possibilities for car design.
   1. Automobiles—Juvenile literature. [1. Automobiles.] I. Title.
TL147.H27   1988   629.2'222—dc19   88-1827
ISBN 0-89686-376-X

International Standard Book Number:	Library of Congress Catalog Card Number:
0-89686-376-X	88-1827

PHOTO CREDITS

Cover: Buick Motor Division
Ford Motor Company: 7, 8, 12-13, 40, 42
Buick Motor Division: 23, 31, 34, 35
Chrysler Motors: 5, 33, 36, 38-39
FPG International: (T. Campbell) 27
The Bettman Archive, Inc.: 11, 15, 16-17, 18, 20-21, 24

Macmillan Publishing Company
866 Third Avenue
New York, NY 10022
Collier Macmillan Canada, Inc.

CRESTWOOD HOUSE

Printed in the United States of America
10   9   8   7   6   5   4   3   2

TABLE OF CONTENTS

AN ELECTRIC DREAM

You're having a dream about the future. Just imagine...you are driving down the road when your car begins to lose power. But you aren't worried. Up ahead, you see a huge blue sign with a yellow lightning streak on it — Streaky's Electric Charge Station. You pull in using the last watt of power in your brand-new Electro-mobile.

The attendant comes out, and you say, "Fill 'er up with high-volt, please. How long will that take?"

"About a minute," he replies.

He removes your worn-out battery and puts in a freshly-charged one. The new battery was in someone else's car earlier today. And your battery will go into another car as soon as it's charged up and ready to provide power.

Then you're off and running, quietly and pollution-free, for another hundred miles.

Sure, you've been dreaming. But your dream may come true in the future. Today's "Dream Car" often becomes tomorrow's reality.

BUILDING A DREAM

Every car is a "Dream Car." Every car you've ever seen started out as someone's dream. These dreamers were able to take their ideas and put them on paper.

4

The Plymouth Slingshot has the unique look of a Dream Car.

They took the ideas they wrote down or drew and made detailed, working models of their dreams. Then they took their models and created full-scale, working automobiles. They saw their dreams come true and were soon driving around in their own "Dream Cars."

Even Henry Ford, the great American automobile inventor, was "dreaming" when he began to work on his first car. Many others followed Ford's lead and improved on his ideas. Soon the automobile became part of the American Dream.

But Ford himself was building on the dreams of others. The world had been going through many changes ever since the 1700s in England. Before that time, when people needed something, they made it themselves, or they got along without it. Then people began working together to make things to sell to other people. The first factories were created. People invented machines that could make many of the same products to sell to the public. This was the beginning of the Industrial Revolution. The age of machines soon spread to Germany and then to the "New World," the United States.

Machines were being made to do many things. It wasn't long before someone came up with the idea of a machine to move people. Trains were the first popular means of mechanical transportation. But some dreamers wanted to create a machine to move individuals rather than crowds. This was how the idea of the car was born.

Today we are in the middle of other kinds of "revolutions." The Electronic, Technological, and Computer Revolutions are changing our lives. They are also changing the way we are building and designing cars.

We can only make educated guesses about what cars will be like in the future. Who knows what discoveries will be made in the next few years, and how these discoveries may change the way we design, build, and power automobiles? Henry Ford could not foresee inventions such as plastic, seatbelts, or computers. Look how those inventions have changed Ford's automobile! The people who are designing cars today or thinking about designs for cars of the

No one really knows what cars of the future will look like, but they could be like Ford's Probe V.

future can only guess at the amazing things that will be available to tomorrow's car builders.

The only thing we know for certain is that there will always be dreamers to think up Dream Cars!

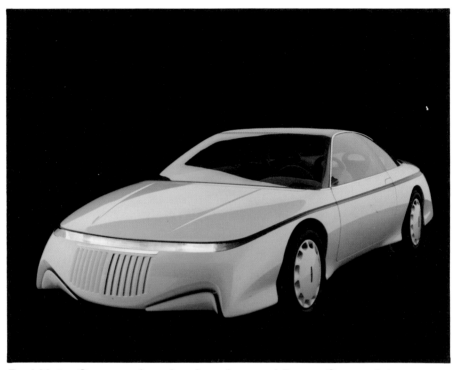
Ford Motor Company has developed several Dream Car models, including The Machete.

DRIVING IN THE FUTURE

What does the future hold? How are cars and driving going to change?

Many people today are worried about the pollution caused by cars. The carbon monoxide given off as a waste product of internal combustion engines is deadly. In most cases, once this exhaust comes out of a car's tailpipe, it is spread out through the rest of the air and becomes harmless. However, where there are many, many cars in a single area, such as in the center of a large city, the amount of carbon monoxide being mixed with the air may become dangerous. The cars may produce too much carbon monoxide for the air to handle.

This is why many city governments are thinking about banning cars from their cities. In the future, you may not be allowed to drive a gas-powered car within a city. You may have to park in one of the huge parking areas at a city's edge and take electric-powered mass transit, such as buses, subways, or monorails into the city. Trucks or trains delivering goods into the city would have to be solar- or electric-powered as well.

Many different power sources are being studied today. Some are new; some are old, abandoned sources from the past. These include nuclear power, solar power, wind power, and steam generators using power from the molten core of the earth. Some engineers are even studying how to use recycled garbage and other waste products in the Dream Cars of tomorrow.

All of the major auto manufacturers have Dream Cars on their drawing boards. Their names sound like dreams of a science fiction writer. The Chrysler Portofino can travel at 150 miles (241 kilometers) per hour. The Pontiac Pursuit is completely controlled by a computer. The Oldsmobile Aerotech holds the world's closed-course speed record. The Chevrolet Express gets 25 miles (40 km) to the gallon of fuel while moving at a cruising speed of 150 miles (241 km) per hour. Ford Probe V has holographic instrument displays. That is, the instruments are three-dimensional images — an advancement over the computer dashes already common today.

Even if none of the predictions scientists are making today about cars comes true, there is still one fact that will remain — there will be changes in the future. The cars that people are dreaming about today may not be the exact one traveling the highways of the next century, but these designs will certainly affect future cars.

Speaking of highways, maybe there won't *be* any in tomorrow's world! One of today's Dream Cars is an air car with powerful fans taking the place of wheels. This kind of Dream Car wouldn't need roads of any sort. In fact, it could even travel on water!

DREAM CARS OF THE PAST

Nobody knows exactly when the dream of the automobile began. The first vehicle ever built that moved on its own power (instead of being pulled by an animal) was only a toy created by the great English scientist Sir Isaac Newton. Newton's toy was a steam car that was pushed forward by a jet of steam. Over the years, many other scientists and inventors created steam cars.

Early steam cars were bulky—and dangerous.

During these years others were working on internal combustion engines. These engines ran by igniting, or setting fire to, certain gases and causing tiny explosions inside a small chamber. The force from these explosions caused a metal shaft to turn. A Dutch scientist named Christian Huygens had

Ford's Probe V is made to move fast and look good.

made the first working internal combustion engine way back in 1687. It was very primitive and no one could find a practical application for it. It wasn't until 1876, almost 200 years later, that a German scientist named Nikolaus August Otto perfected the kind of internal combustion engine on which most modern engines are based. In the United States, brothers Charles and Frank Duryea brought out the first "horseless carriage" in 1894, using a two-cylinder internal combustion engine. Henry Ford introduced his first car in 1896.

Even though he was not the first inventor to dream up a way to build a car, Henry Ford is considered the "inventor" of the automobile. This is probably because of the way his cars were built. Using a moving belt called a conveyor belt, Ford's automobile factory became the fastest at putting cars together. It didn't take long before there were more Ford cars than any other kind on American roads. Henry Ford was able to make the dream of thousands of Americans come true. He wanted everyone to have a Dream Car! Henry Ford's Model 'T' is recognized around the world as the first practical automobile. As the years went by, many other people's dreams led to the fast, efficient, safe, and beautiful cars we know today.

Today, automobile designers are constantly working to improve the performance, safety features, and the "look" of the Dream Cars of tomorrow.

"Nearly a Quarter-Century of Leadership"
The Stevens-Duryea is the most imitated motor-car in America.
This is true recognition of its leadership for nearly a Quarter-Century.
Limousines and Berlines $5750 to $6200
Stevens-Duryea Company Chicopee Falls Mass   "Pioneer Builders of American Sixes"

The Stevens-Duryea was one of the first "horseless carriages" in the United States.

Early "Dream Cars" were painted black and built to look like horse carriages.

16

DESIGNING CARS OF THE FUTURE

Henry Ford's Model 'T' allowed many Americans to own a car during the 1920s. His assembly line helped lower the cost of building cars, so he was able to sell his cars for a lower price. In the 1920s almost 20 million Americans became car owners.

During the same period, other motor companies thought that many Americans would want a car

Henry Ford's 1922 Model 'T' sold for only $415.00.

more expensive than the ones driven by the "average" citizens. These other car manufacturers felt that there was a market for "classy" cars. It was their dream to make these Dream Cars available for rich and famous people. This was the beginning of car "design."

The "father" of car design was a man named Harley Earl. He began his career designing Dream Cars for Hollywood movie stars. Each one was custom-made — completely different from any other. At the time, most car builders were modeling their automobiles after old horse carriages. Earl invented "streamlining." His idea was to make his cars look like they were speeding by even when they were standing still! His new ideas worked. Each car he built was long, low, and sleek. It looked as if it could beat any other car on the road in a race. Earl was also making cars in different colors. Before this, all cars were black.

General Motors (GM) heard of Earl's work and hired him to design cars for them. GM was one of the companies that wanted to develop a line of "classy" Dream Cars. Earl was in charge of the General Motors styling section from 1927 to 1959. During that time, over 50 million cars were made by General Motors, all designed by Earl. He believed that cars were not just machines to move people around but also objects of beauty. He believed that cars should attract customers by their appearance *and*

Actor Walter Pidgeon poses with his brand new 1930 Cadillac.

20

performance.

One of the most important things Earl realized was that changing the shape of a car's body could affect the way it moved. The more the wind pushed on the car, the more difficult it was for the car to go forward. This is why designers began creating fins on the Dream Cars. The fins were originally designed to help cars move faster with less wind resistance (pushing from the air). The more designers and research scientists learned about how body shape affected a car's performance, the more changes they made.

Today, designers begin by making hundreds of sketches of new car designs. Scientists study these until they determine which is the best possible design for beauty and performance. Next, they create a model of the car out of clay. These first models are made 1:5 scale. This means that every inch of the model equals five inches of a full-sized car. These clay models are placed in a wind tunnel to see how moving air affects them. Changes are made to perfect the model. The next step is to make a full-scale clay model! This takes hundreds of pounds of clay and many weeks of work. Once the final body has passed the tests, production can finally begin.

Today, automobile designers are using the most advanced technology. They learn the best body shape for style, safety, and performance for future Dream Cars. These specialists are looking to the future. But they have to thank men of the past like Harley Earl for paving the road that leads to tomorrow!

The Buick Wildcat is another "Dream Car" being developed for the roads of the future.

THE "DREAM" STEAM CAR

Some Dream Cars of the future may be powered by steam. That's a pretty funny idea, because some of the first cars ever invented were steam cars. Way back in 1769, Nicholas Joseph Cugnot (pronounced KOO-NYOH) made the first full-sized steam Dream Car.

THE FASTEST CAR IN THE WORLD
(Rate of 127.66 Miles an Hour)

For a few months in 1898, the "Stanley Steamer" was the most popular Dream Car.

Cugnot attached a high-pressure boiler to a shaft and attached the shaft to the wheels of his car. The boiler would build up pressure. When the pressure was released under control, it would turn the shaft which would turn the wheels. Then Cugnot would "race" down the road — at a top speed of two and a half miles (four km) per hour!

Unfortunately, early steam cars had a major problem. Sometimes the high-pressure boilers would build up too much pressure and would explode. Because of this defect, laws were passed in England forbidding steam cars from driving on British roads.

Cugnot's car had another problem. He could get it to move forward just fine, but he couldn't always stop it. One time he collided with a wall and knocked it over. This was the first car accident!

Other inventors improved on Cugnot's model.

One of the most famous of these inventors was F. E. Stanley. The "Stanley Steamer" won an important race in 1898. After the race more than 200 people ordered their own Steamers. But Stanley and his brother, who built their cars by hand, couldn't possibly fill all of the orders.

Steam cars never became very popular. People had more faith in railroads and stagecoaches for travel than in cars, and they also feared that the steam-powered cars might blow up.

Then in 1967 car designers began to think seriously about using steam to power cars again. They were concerned about air pollution. New studies by private and governmental groups showed that steam power could be practical for use in automobiles and would not spew dangerous exhaust fumes into the air. Many people were against the idea. They were remembering the old steam engines that would take a long time to start in cold weather or that would freeze up altogether. They said that steam engines would be too heavy, too complicated, too expensive, and would not allow cars to travel very far on a tank of fuel.

But many technical people who had been working on steam engines pointed out that there was a lot of new technology. Modern steam engines could be much safer and more powerful than the engines built more than a century ago. The modern steam systems would allow a steam car to equal the speed of a gasoline-powered car and travel about 30 miles (48 km) per gallon of kerosene or diesel oil. Modern steam systems use the same water over and over again. The driver would need to fill the tank only after many trips. These steam systems are also sealed very tightly, making higher pressure in a smaller space. They are able to start up in nine or ten seconds under normal conditions. In cold weather, they can start up in 20 seconds or less.

Steam engines also have fewer moving parts than internal combustion engines. This means that there are fewer needed repairs.

Work continues on steam engines, and the Dream Cars of tomorrow may be powered on a dream of yesterday.

ELECTRIC DREAM CARS

For a short time, electric cars were more popular in the United States than gas-powered cars. People in American cities were familiar with electric trolley cars and trains. The inventors of these vehicles had developed many different batteries and motors. Thomas Edison, one of the greatest American inventors, had created the Edison Cell, a nickel-iron battery which was the most popular for electric car use.

Henry Ford's ability to mass produce his internal combustion cars was once again the main reason electric cars did not catch on at the beginning of automotive history. However, the same concerns about air pollution caused by the internal combustion engine have led modern car designers back to electric power.

Today, every major auto manufacturer is examining the possibility of electric Dream Cars for the future. Some are already in use today. The Lunar

Because of Henry Ford's early development, today's cars are mass produced rapidly.

Rover, built by the Boeing Aerospace Company for use on the moon, is an electrically-powered car.

There are many different types of electric motors. Most of them operate in the same way. Early scientists discovered that similar magnetic poles repel each other and unlike poles attract. Electricity moves through electric wires from negative to positive, forming what is called a circuit. When this happens, the wire becomes an electromagnet, with a negative and positive side. In an electric motor a battery is connected to a wire and the wire is placed into a magnet. The wire is continually repelled and attracted by the magnet, making it spin. When connected to a shaft, this turning motion can make anything spin, including the wheels of a car!

Of course, much of the normal internal combustion gas cars of today use batteries. But these are not used to make the car move. They are used for electric starters, headlights, heating and cooling systems, radios, and cigarette lighters. Much more powerful and longer-lasting batteries will be needed to power an entire car.

Just imagine what it would be like if such cars were available for the average person. You would see the familiar gas station replaced by electric charge stations. Or maybe electric chargers will be on city streets like parking meters. While you're parked, your car is hooked up to the city's electric generators, and you're charged for power on your monthly electric bill.

SOLAR DREAM CARS

What is the greatest source of power on the Earth? It's the sun! The rays we feel that give off heat and light are actually radiant power streaming from the sun 93 million miles (143 million km) away. This power from the sun is very dangerous. Luckily, the upper region of our planet's atmosphere is made of ozone, a blue chemical which is actually a form of oxygen. This ozone layer filters out most of the harmful rays of the sun.

In 1954, scientists began experimenting with solar cells which were able to make electricity from the sun's rays. In the future these new solar cells would work as well as some of the most modern steam and gas engines.

In 1974, the United States government sponsored many research programs in solar energy. They wanted to speed up scientific development of solar power. In most cases, scientists working with solar energy are looking for ways to make cheaper heating for homes and for hot water supplies. However, the designers of the future are already working on the creation of a solar-powered Dream Car!

Just imagine — a solar-powered car would never

have to stop at a gas station. Drivers would never have to worry about running out of gas. They wouldn't have to stay at home on cloudy or rainy days, either. The batteries being developed for solar cars save up the sun's rays during sunny days so that the power can be used later for cloudy days and at night. If every car were solar-powered, there would be no gas stations and no air pollution from cars. Also, there would be an unlimited source of power. Scientists tell us that the sun will continue to burn for millions and millions of years.

Solar power is already being considered for use in some cars today. It is now possible to have a solar battery installed in the roof of your car that would automatically switch on your air conditioner. This device is designed so that your car's interior would never become over heated, even if you have to leave it parked in the sun.

The same solar battery could charge up your car's battery on a cold morning so you would be able to start up your car in the worst snow storms.

The only thing holding up the popular use of solar engines is money. The systems that are ready now are very expensive and do not produce enough power to run cars for long. But the more scientists dream, the more ideas they come up with. As long as they continue to research the possibilities of solar power, the more chances there are for solar cars to be among the Dream Cars of the future.

Buick displays its newest Dream Car, the Questor.

TESTING THE FUTURE'S DREAM CARS

Millions of people love to watch auto races. These races are not just tests of speed. Car manufacturers use these races to test their new engines and equipment. Racing cars are usually covered with decals and names of well-known car equipment manufacturers. These companies are not just supporting the car in order to advertise their name. In most cases, they have donated much of the equipment on these race cars. They have helped with everything — from the tires, to the engine, to the body of the car. They have helped to develop the safety features from seatbelts to the driver's helmet and racing suit.

They use the races to test their equipment under the toughest conditions. If their equipment can stand up to the dangers of a race track, then it will surely stand up under normal driving conditions.

Most car manufacturers have their own test tracks which duplicate all kinds of road conditions. They can simulate any kind of weather conditions on these test tracks, too. They can make it rain, or they can make the road slippery with ice. They have made sections of track with potholes and dirt to see if their new cars can travel in the worst places.

The Dream Car makers work in the laboratory, too. They use the most modern technology to test their cars, from the windows to the radio. They have automatic equipment that opens and closes doors hundreds of times a day. They crash the cars against brick walls to see how safe the driver and passengers will be in an accident.

The more modern the car, the rougher the tests. Each new development must pass tests that all the cars before it have passed. The tests are designed to discover the limits of each piece of equipment. If something fails a test, the automotive engineers study it more to see why it failed. Once they learn that, they return to their drawing boards and try to make

The streamlined console of the Plymouth Slingshot.

the next one pass. In this way, car manufacturers are working their way towards the cars of the future. Every car you see on the road today has gone through hundreds of tests to make certain it runs properly. The engineers also get reports from people driving the company's cars and from independent study groups.

No one really knows how the cars of the future will be tested. With each new advancement, scientists are creating new tests. These new tests will help them create the safest, most economical and most attractive Dream Cars for tomorrow.

Map displays like the one in the Buick Wildcat will prevent drivers of the future from getting lost.

COMPUTERS AND DREAM CARS

Only a few decades ago, computers were believed to be tools only for the very smartest scientists. However, with the advancements made in the computer industry, many of the people in the United States now know how to work a computer.

Computers are being used to design every aspect of cars today. Naturally, they are also hard at work helping design the cars of tomorrow, too. Scientists

Computer displays dominate the inside of the Buick Questor.

use computers to design car engines and bodies. Every bit of information they gather through study and testing is entered into their computers. The results are displayed at a speed and with an accuracy undreamed of just a few years ago. Computers are the reason that advancements in car design are coming so rapidly.

Many engines are equipped with diagnostic computers that allow auto mechanics to hook up the engine to their own computers. This way, mechanics can learn if there is a mechanical problem with the car.

The futuristic interior of the Plymouth Slingshot.

The Dream Cars of the future, as far as the computer experts are concerned, will be computer cars! Not only will they have computers in their dashboards and engines, but they will also have directional computers. These machines will have built-in electronic maps, so drivers will never get lost. There will be computers to control the temperature of the car, so the engine will never become overheated and the passengers will always be comfortable.

Computers will also be able to improve the safety of cars. Some computers will prevent cars from starting if seat belts are not fastened or if the driver has been drinking too much!

Dream Cars of tomorrow, like some cars today, will be bought using computers. Automotive manufacturers will program all the details about their new cars into a computer network. People with home computers will link up to this network with their telephones. They'll be able to examine each aspect of the new car, from the interior to the body. They'll be able to see the inside of the engine and how it works. They'll also be able to review all of the testing results the manufacturers have collected.

The use for computers in cars is limited only by the imaginations of automotive designers. With all the advancements we've seen in the past ten years alone, it would appear that the sky is the limit!

The Chrysler Portofino can travel at very high speeds, but looks just as good when it's standing still.

SAFETY IN DREAM CARS

Using different ways to power the Dream Cars of tomorrow might be the best way of making the cars safer for the environment. At the same time, many concerned designers and scientists are looking for ways to make the cars of the future (and today) safer for drivers and passengers. Thousands of people are hurt or killed in automobile accidents every year. Many of these injuries could have been prevented if

the cars had been safer. The changes being made in cars to improve safety will affect the designs of Dream Cars of the future.

In 1965, a lawyer named Ralph Nader published a book called *Unsafe At Any Speed.* The book reported that many American cars were quite dangerous. Nader's Dream Car put driver and passenger safety ahead of performance and style. His work led auto makers to pay more attention to safety in cars.

Many states have passed seat belt laws which state that persons driving or riding in cars must wear seat belts. Scientists and safety experts have been studying seat belts for years. Their studies have shown that seat belts save thousands of lives each year.

Another safety feature which may be installed in all the Dream Cars of the future is the air bag. This is a plastic bag located underneath the dashboard which instantly inflates upon impact, protecting the driver from injury. Air bags are not yet standard features on cars, but they may be a requirement in the cars of the future. The Dream Cars of tomorrow promise to be the safest cars ever made.

The classic-looking Ford Quicksilver.

There's a big difference between the Dream Cars of yesterday and the Dream Cars of today!

DESIGNING YOUR OWN DREAM CAR

You are dreaming again, thinking up your own Dream Car. How will it look? How will it drive? What special features will it have?

No one knows what the future holds, but here's a chance for you to make your own predictions —

about your own Dream Car.

Will your car be long and sleek or short and compact? Will it be powered by gasoline, electricity, steam, solar energy, nuclear power, or some other (as yet) unknown source?

Will it roll on tires or hover above the ground on jets of air? Will it be made of steel, plastic, or some lightweight metal? Will computers handle the driving while you sit back and enjoy the ride?

How fast will it run? How far will you be able to travel on one load of fuel? How many miles will you be able to travel before your car wears out and you have to buy another Dream Car?

How safe will your car be? What safety features will it contain?

There you have it — your very own Dream Car. It's a beauty.

FOR MORE INFORMATION

For more information about Dream Car research and manufacturing, write to:

Popular Mechanics
Hearst Corporation
959 Eighth Avenue
New York, NY 10019

Road and Track
P.O. Box 5331
1255 Portland Place
Boulder, CO 18749

GLOSSARY/INDEX

AIR BAGS 41 — *A safety feature in automobiles. Air bags are made of an inflatable plastic bag that inflates on impact to protect the driver and passengers.*

AIR CARS 10 — *Cars of the future designed to ride on cushions of air generated by large fans on the car's underside.*

CUGNOT, NICHOLAS JOSEPH 23, 24 — *A Frenchman credited with the invention of the first steam car in 1769.*

DURYEA, CHARLES AND FRANK 14 — *Brothers who, in 1894, invented the first "horseless carriage" using an internal combustion engine.*

EARL, HARLEY 19, 23 — *The "father" of modern automotive design.*

EDISON CELL 26 — *The electric battery invented by Thomas Edison which was the most popular means of power for the early electric cars.*

EDISON, THOMAS 26 — *The American inventor whose inventions include the electric light bulb and the Edison Cell electric battery.*

ELECTRIC CARS 26, 27, 28 — *Any road vehicle that uses electricity for its main source of power.*

FORD, HENRY 5, 6, 7, 14, 18, 27 — *The American inventor who is often called the "inventor" of the car. His real success came because of his use of*

GLOSSARY / INDEX

mass production to lower the cost of building cars so he could make his cars available to everyone.

HORSELESS CARRIAGE 14 — *The early name for automobiles.*

HUYGENS, CHRISTIAN 11 — *A Dutch scientist who built the first working internal combustion engine in 1687.*

INDUSTRIAL REVOLUTION 6 — *The movement which began the invention and use of machines to create products for many people. This took the place of the old method of everyone creating what they needed at home. The Industrial Revolution began in England in the 1700s.*

INTERNAL COMBUSTION ENGINE 8, 11, 14, 27 — *Any engine which uses the force from the explosion of gases inside a chamber to turn a driveshaft.*

MODEL 'T' 14, 18 — *The first "practical" automobile invented by Henry Ford.*

NADER, RALPH 41 — *Author of* Unsafe At Any Speed, *the book that led to better safety features on all American cars.*

NEWTON, SIR ISAAC 11 — *The English scientist who is credited with the invention of the first self-propelled vehicle, a steam model.*

OTTO, NIKOLAUS 14 — *A German scientist who,*

GLOSSARY/INDEX

in 1876, perfected the kind of internal combustion engine on which most modern engines are based.

SOLAR CARS 29, 30 — *Any road vehicle that uses solar energy for its main source of power.*

STANLEY, F. E. 25 — *An inventor who, in 1898, built the "Stanley Steamer," the most popular of the steam cars.*

STEAM CARS 11, 23, 24, 25 — *Any road vehicle that uses steam for its main source of power.*

WIND TUNNEL 22 — *A device used by scientists to test wind resistance against vehicles.*